CCSS Genre Fantasy

MW00570460

Essential Question
How can you make new friends feel welcome?

Cara and the Sky Kingdom

by Eirlys Hunter
illustrated by Chris Jevons

"Hurry up, Hal, or we'll miss the welcoming ceremony," called Mina.

Hal pushed the manual starter on his cloudster again, and this time it purred to life. The twins raced their cloudsters to catch up with their parents, and they all joined the throng of people entering City Hall.

Most of Staria seemed to have come to see the new ruler. A trumpeter blew a fanfare, and then the Royal Council marched onto the stage.

"This is an extremely special occasion," said the chief councillor. "The Royal Council has traveled to many planets to locate the heir to the Starian throne, so please welcome Princess Cara!"

A gasp ran through the crowd, and Mina, leaning forward to get a better view, saw a small figure walk uncertainly into the spotlight.

The new ruler was a human! She was a very young human wearing a Starian cloak.

"Princess Cara's uncle was our dear king, whose recent death was such a devastating blow," the chief councillor said. "Years ago, Cara's father journeyed to Earth and married a human. Her father is also dead, and because Cara is his daughter, she inherits the throne and is our new princess!"

Cara stepped forward. "Thank you," she said in a trembling voice. "I'm afraid I only found out recently that Staria existed. I hope that you will be patient as I learn your customs."

Someone called out, "How can she rule Staria when she's only a child?"

Someone else shouted, "Can she control the weather?"

"I welcome you on behalf of the people of Staria!" the chief councillor announced. He extended his hands to grasp her elbows, but Cara took his right hand and shook it. This caused a lot of laughter because Cara didn't know how to greet in the Starian way.

The opening bars of the national anthem began, and everyone raised their arms to sing "Oh Staria, Oh Staria, We Love Our Kingdom Fair." Everyone, that is, except Cara.

Hal snorted scornfully. "Don't they have any respect on Earth?"

The ceremony finished with a short play where an actor playing the old king zipped around on his cloudster, using his powers to keep away the wind and ice.

"Has Cara inherited the king's powers?" muttered Mina's father. "That's all we want to know."

Several days later, Hal and Mina were helping in their parents' bakery.

"Can we go to the recycling center now?" Hal asked. "I need a new starter board for my cloudster."

"Soon," their father said, scooping batter into tins.

Mina was stacking moonglow tarts. "Have you heard anything about Cara?" she asked.

"Praxti has been hired by the palace to help Cara settle in," replied their mother, sliding a tray of cookies into the oven. "Apparently, Cara's finding it difficult to adjust. Praxti just tele-whispered to say that she wants you two to help her."

"Us?" spluttered Hal through a mouthful of pastry.

"She wants you to show Cara around. Praxti thinks Cara needs some Starian friends her own age to help her get used to her new life here. You can visit the palace on the way to the recycling center."

"Wow! I'm nervous!" Mina said. "How do you talk to a princess?"

"Don't forget, she's not used to being a princess yet," said her father. "Just be yourselves."

The twins found Praxti in the palace garden with Cara, who was dribbling a black and white ball around.

"Cara, meet Mina and Hal. They're cloudster experts, and they're going to teach you how to ride your cloudster and take you on a tour of the dome."

"We are?" Mina asked.

"You are," Praxti said firmly. "I've explained that the glass dome protects the city, and Cara has expressed an interest in seeing it."

Cara picked up her ball. "Can you really teach me to ride a cloudster?" she asked shyly. "It looks fun."

The twins showed Cara how to control her breath so that her cloudster started as she approached it, and then they showed her how to jump on.

Cara started riding the cloudster cautiously, moving slowly and stopping often, but soon she was whizzing around the garden.

"Hey, you're a natural!" Hal said.

"Off you go," Praxti said, "and Cara, pull your hood up over your hair, or people will stare at you. Unless it's cut, human hair keeps growing," she explained to the twins.

"I wish my hair grew like yours," Mina said admiringly.

"First stop, the recycling center," Hal said.

They swooped out of the gate and whooshed past the news-beam collection point to the mountain of abandoned cloudsters at the recycling plant. Humming happily, Hal poked around in the jumble of parts.

"His favorite activities are scrounging for parts and riding his cloudster," Mina said.

Cara nodded but didn't reply, and Mina was concerned. "I'm sorry, Princess Cara," she said, "am I being too familiar?"

Cara looked up. "No, it's just that everything here is so different from home."

"What's your favorite game on Earth?" Mina asked.

"Soccer," Cara said. "Do you play?"

Mina shook her head. She'd never heard of it.

"Perhaps I could teach you?" Cara asked, smiling.

"I'd love that," Mina replied.

"I've found one!" Hal yelled excitedly, clutching a starter board he'd just found.

On the way back to the palace, the twins showed Cara the field where they played games on their cloudsters. Then they took her past the hanging-food gardens.

"What's that delicious smell?" Cara asked as they floated past a stall.

"Roasted pillownuts," Hal replied.

"We make pillownut cakes in our bakery, and I hope you'll try them," Mina said. She tele-whispered their mother that they were bringing Cara for a visit. Their mother said she'd let Praxti know.

Their parents greeted Cara at the bakery door by touching her elbows and closing their eyes.

The bakery smelled of the glorious sweet spiciness of the freshly baked pillownut cakes that Mina handed around.

Cara bit into one and grinned. "That's probably the yummiest thing I've ever tasted!" she announced.

Freshly Baked

Roasted Pillownut Cakes

Cloudberry Pies

Moonglow Tarts

The twins insisted that Cara taste the cloudberry pies and moonglow tarts, too. "Yum!" cooed Cara.

Soon Praxti arrived. "I heard thunder on the way over," she whispered to their mother.

Their mother frowned. "Mina, why don't you show Cara your cloudster awards?"

Mina was puzzled that her mother didn't want them to overhear the adults' conversation, but she didn't say anything.

Cara admired the awards that Mina and Hal had won for cloudster bumping.

"How do you play cloudster bumping?" asked Cara.

"There are two teams, and you start in your own half and try to cross the other team's line," replied Mina. "If you get bumped off the side of the field, you have to stay off until that round has finished."

"Do you ever get injured?" Cara asked.

"No, because if you fall, you just land in the cloudster's softness. The cloudster stops moving when you lose your balance."

"You and Hal make a powerful team," Cara said. "Is it because you're twins?"

"Maybe. Mom says we have complementary abilities. I'm imaginative, and Hal's logical. I'm creative, and he's practical."

"Cloudster bumping sounds awesome," said Cara. "Can I play sometime?"

"We'll take you to a game tomorrow," Mina told her.

Suddenly there was a flash of lightning, then a clap of thunder in the distance, and Mina shivered.

"Mina, why were your mother and Praxti whispering before?"

Mina decided to be honest. "Staria has terrible storms, which is why the kingdom's under a dome. Since the king died, everyone's been nervous because he had special powers that controlled the weather and protected us."

"So I'm expected to control storms?" Cara said, looking terrified.

Mina bit her lip. "I'm afraid so," she replied.

After Praxti had taken Cara home, their mother smiled at the twins. "It must be tough for your new friend."

"She's an acquaintance," Hal replied. "You can't be friends with a princess."

"Yes, you can," Mina said. "Plus, she's lonely, and she doesn't know our customs, so she needs real friends."

CHAPTER 4 Cara's Challenge

The next morning, when Mina and Hal picked up Cara from the palace, she was wearing her hair tucked under a cap.

Mina and Hal showed Cara how to ride her cloudster standing up, with one leg behind the other.

"Wow, it's just like surfing!" Cara said.

"What's surfing?" Hal asked.

"It's an Earth sport that I'm certain you'd love."

When they arrived at the field, the twins' friends were excited to meet Cara, who remembered to close her eyes as their elbows touched.

The bumping field was a long rectangle with a back line marked in red at one end and another in blue at the other end. The group divided into two teams, four players on each side. Cara was on Mina's team, and their goal was to cross the red line while keeping Hal's team away from the blue line.

They all stood on their cloudsters, and Hal yelled, "Round one, go!" They all leaned forward, and the two teams raced toward each other. Mina rammed Hal from the side, but although he wobbled, he didn't lose his balance.

Next, Mina and Cara teamed up to bump their cloudsters into Mina's friend Zendi, and together they shunted her right over the sideline.

"Yes!" Mina whooped.

Then Hal and another member of his team joined up to bump Mina off the field, leaving space for Cara. She dodged away, shooting down the field and over the red line.

"This game is amazing!" Cara shouted to Mina. Her eyes were sparkling as she steered down the field to wait for the next round to begin.

Just then a warning bell began to toll, and everyone looked up nervously.

"What is it?" Cara asked.

"It's a storm warning," Hal said grimly.

As Hal spoke, lightning flickered through the sky, and a loud thunderclap followed almost immediately.

People began pouring onto the field, some on foot and others on their cloudsters. Parents clutched their children, and everyone looked up apprehensively at the sky beyond the dome.

Because of the dome, Mina couldn't feel or hear the powerful wind, but she could see the lightning coming closer and feel the claps of thunder that shook the ground.

The twins' parents arrived, and Mina's mother hugged her tightly. The ground beyond the dome was turning white, and the sky above it was gray. Giant balls of ice larger than Mina's head were hurtling out of the sky and bouncing into huge icy piles.

"The dome will never survive if one of those hailstones hits it," murmured the twins' father, putting an arm around Hal's shoulders.

The swirling ice came closer and closer, and a hailstone rolled right up to the dome. Then Mina noticed Cara wasn't there. "Hey! Look at what Cara's doing!" she shouted.

Everyone watched. Cara was standing on her cloudster, making it spin faster and faster in tight circles. Her cap flew off, and her hair whipped across her face as she spun around.

Cara continued spinning with her arms stretched out while Mina hid her face in her mother's chest.

"This is the worst storm ever!" Hal shouted.

Then he heard someone gasp, and he looked up. Had the dome cracked? No—the sky was actually brightening, the hail had stopped, and the clouds were retreating. Soon the sun began shining and melting the giant hailstones that lay just beyond the dome.

Gradually Cara slowed down her cloudster and then flopped into it, exhausted, while Mina and Hal ran to congratulate her.

"You did it! You saved Staria!"

"How did you know what to do?" Hal asked.

Cara laughed. "I'm not sure. Maybe it was instinct, but I just knew what to do somehow."

Everyone was hugging one another with delight and relief. The dome was safe, and Cara had proven that she was the rightful ruler of Staria.

The twins jumped onto their cloudsters and accompanied Cara, grinning and waving, on a lap of the field while the crowd cheered and waved.

After the applause died down, Mina pointed to Cara's soccer ball. "I think it's time we learned to play your game now," she said.

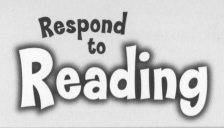

Respond to Reading

Summarize

Use important details from *Cara and the Sky Kingdom* to summarize the story. Your graphic organizer may help you.

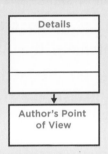

Details

↓

Author's Point of View

Text Evidence

1. What features tell you that *Cara and the Sky Kingdom* is a fantasy? **GENRE**

2. What is the narrator's point of view in this story? Use two examples from the text to explain how you know. **POINT OF VIEW**

3. What does the word *apprehensively* on page 13 mean? Use the clues in the paragraph to help you figure out its meaning. **PARAGRAPH CLUES**

4. Write about how the story would change if it were written from a different point of view. **WRITE ABOUT READING**

Compare Texts

Read about a man who makes new friends and learns new skills.

Robin Hood's Great Friend

Robin Hood hurried through Sherwood Forest. Suddenly his path was blocked by a deep stream. He decided to cross where a wide tree trunk had fallen over the stream and created a bridge.

Robin Hood noticed a giant of a man, as tall and broad as an oak tree, on the other end of the bridge.

"Let me pass!" Robin called.

"No, you let me pass," the man said, raising his staff.

Within moments, the men were clashing staffs, and then the stranger pushed Robin into the water.

Robin Hood climbed out, dripping wet. He blew his horn, and his Merry Men appeared with their bows drawn, ready to fight the giant.

"Wait!" Robin shouted. He turned to the man. "I am Robin Hood," he said.

"Robin Hood!" the stranger said, grinning. "My name is John Little. I want to join your band of Merry Men. I promise I will prove trustworthy."

Robin smiled and held out his hand. He knew this man was just what their group required, so he instructed his Merry Men to take their new friend back to their forest hideout.

The Merry Men prepared a feast to welcome John Little. Robin told John Little how the Sheriff of Nottingham had driven him from his house and land.

"The Sheriff and King John are seizing all the land, and now many families are starving. When wealthy travelers pass through the forest, we invite them to eat with us."

"We feed them well," Maid Marion added.

"Yes, we give them dinner, and then we tell them they must pay for it," Robin said. "We donate the money to the starving villagers."

"The Sheriff is determined to catch us," Friar Tuck said, "but we have fun outwitting him."

"Is this forest dangerous?" John Little asked.

"The only danger comes from the Sheriff's soldiers," Robin said. "We'll teach you how to move silently so you can take them by surprise."

"Can you also teach me how to shoot a straight arrow?" John Little asked.

"With pleasure!" Robin said. "In return, will you teach us how to fight with a staff?"

John Little gladly agreed. Then Robin said, "You need a new name. In the forest, I'm not Robin Locksley but Robin Hood. Your name should be Little John."

Little John agreed, and Maid Marion said, "Let's hear it for our new friend, the biggest little man we've ever seen!"

Make Connections

How did sharing skills help John Little develop new friendships in *Robin Hood's Great Friend*? ESSENTIAL QUESTION

How do the new friendships that people make in both stories enrich their communities? TEXT TO TEXT

Focus on Genre

Fantasy Fantasy fiction has features that wouldn't happen in real life. Some fantasy fiction is set in ancient worlds with dragons and treasures. Other fantasy stories have a modern setting and may include talking animals or unreal creatures that have special powers.

Read and Find Reread the descriptions of Cara's new home. Identify the main differences between her new home and her home on Earth. How believable is the world the author has created?

Your Turn

Work in a group to turn a scene from *Cara and the Sky Kingdom* into a drama. You'll need to figure out how to show that her new home is different from Earth and how to make cloudsters. Remember to focus on the way Cara and the twins get to know each other and share their different abilities.